" . . . and BE BAPTIZED"

"...and BE BAPTIZED"

A Minister's Handbook on Baptism

By KENNETH IRVING BROWN

PHILADELPHIA

THE JUDSON PRESS

CHICAGO   LOS ANGELES

Now when they heard this, they were pricked in their heart, and said unto Peter and to the rest of the apostles, Men and brethren, what shall we do?

Then Peter said unto them, Repent, and be baptized every one of you in the name of Jesus Christ for the remission of sins, and ye shall receive the gift of the Holy Ghost. . . .

Then they that gladly received his word were baptized: and the same day there were added unto them about three thousand souls.

—*Acts 2:37-38, 41*

Contents

A Word to the Reader

THIS handbook grew indirectly out of a conversation early in 1947 with Dr. Edwin McNeill Poteat, then president of Colgate-Rochester Divinity School. I was asking why more instruction in the caring for the ordinance of baptism was not given by our seminaries to our ministers-in-training. Out of that conversation came the suggestion of a motion picture training film, intended for use in seminaries and ministerial groups, showing the procedure of immersion as cared for by leaders of our churches, and calling attention specifically to certain practices which are commonly counted undesirable, and by some persons offensive.[1]

In the course of preparing the motion picture, it was suggested by Dr. Benjamin P. Browne, Executive Director of the Division of Christian Publications of the Board of Education and Publication of the American Baptist Convention, that a series of articles on baptism might make more generally available some of the material assembled for the film. At his request a series of five articles was prepared. These articles were published in *Baptist Leader* during 1948. Now, this material, much revised and enlarged, has become the substance of this handbook.

[1] This film, entitled *Customs and Techniques of Baptism,* may now be secured from the Department of Audio-Visual Aids, Council on Missionary Cooperation, American Baptist Convention, 152 Madison Avenue, New York 16, N. Y., or 19 South LaSalle Street, Chicago 3, Ill. It is a forty-minute, silent film, and is restricted to use in theological seminaries and ministers' conferences. There is a nominal service charge. All requests for the film should be accompanied by a letter stating the place, the date, and the group to which it is to be shown.

There is one other word of explanation which possibly should be added. It is my conviction, as will be obvious to the reader, that baptism in New Testament times was by immersion; and, furthermore, that only immersion possesses the symbolic character prescribed by the New Testament. That is to say, it is to be a dramatization of the candidate's death and burial to sin and resurrection to a new and righteous life. Sprinkling or pouring does not convey this significance. The arguments supporting this point of view have been set forth convincingly in numerous books, and for that reason they are not repeated here.

Among the denominations which practice immersion, there are, however, some differences of opinion concerning the purpose for which baptism is administered. Some hold that baptism merely witnesses to a conversion which already has taken place; others hold that baptism is an act of obedience to a divine commandment, and that this obedience is in some way essential to a complete experience of regeneration. Because the questionnaire used in gathering information was sent to a large and representative list of ministers, some reflections of these different theological views very naturally may be discovered in the replies which are quoted. In writing this book, I have limited the discussion, so far as I could, to the techniques connected with the conduct of baptismal services. If certain statements seem to imply a theological bias one way or the other, these implications are inadvertent. They do not represent an attempt to impose a personal theological view upon others.

Long is the list of my friends to whom I am in-
debted for their aid in connection with the motion
picture, the series of articles with their photographs,
and the material in this handbook. I cannot name
them all, but I should be rightly counted ungrateful
if I did not speak my thanks to those who have been
most helpful. It was generous of Dr. Benjamin P.
Browne to allow me to make this further use of the
articles in *Baptist Leader*. The help which Dr.
Browne, the Rev. Raymond L. Bailey, Dr. Clarence
W. Cranford, the Rev. Alfred Nothstein, and Dr.
Harold C. Phillips offered me in the motion picture
was large. I wish to thank also those Denison Uni-
versity students who worked with me in the preparation of the motion picture and the photographs,
particularly David Hart, Lewis Feesler, Tadao
Mukaihata, Eugene Chamberlain, Marilou Taggart,
William F. Connor, Paul C. Mills, Roscoe V. Stuber,
F. William Miller, and Eugene Shellenbarger; and
three other young friends, Jack Whitman, Charles
Russell, and Gordon Roadarmel. I am greatly in-
debted to my friend, Robert N. Back, for his criticism and help in many ways, particularly in the
earlier stages of this endeavor, and to Dr. Edwin T.
Dahlberg for his co-operative aid when the book
was in galley proof.

To all of these, and to a score of others who of
necessity must remain unnamed, I would express
my very sincere appreciation.

If the motion picture, the articles in *Baptist
Leader*, and this handbook play any part in arousing
our ministers to the need of re-examining their
procedures of baptism, if they are of any value in

adding great depth of meaning to their services of baptism, or in increasing the dignity and loveliness of those services, then will my hours of labor be well repaid.

—KENNETH I. BROWN

October 1, 1951
Saint Louis, Missouri

CHAPTER 1

A Preface to Baptism

"Let all things be done decently and in order."
—*1 Corinthians 14:40*

THIS handbook has been prepared in the single-minded hope that it may aid our ministers in making the baptismal service an experience filled with beauty and spiritual power. Much attention is given to such externalities as the minister's robe, the candidate's gown, the cleanliness and temperature of the water; there is emphasis upon the avoidance of any splashing, the rhythm of the act of immersion, the protection of the candidate in his wet garments from the gaze of the congregation. All of these are important items, yet at the very outset this caution needs to be stressed: attention to these details alone can never make baptism all that it should be either to the candidate or to the congregation.

Of first importance, and without them all else is meaningless, are the utter sincerity and reverential attitude of the minister and the candidate. If any minister or any candidate comes to baptism without these, the service may be outwardly impressive, but it will be without significance as an act of worship. However, if the minister, coming to baptism with all reverence and sincerity, is able to care for the many items and niceties which make for dignity, and is careful to avoid those gaucheries which too often mar the service, he has done his utmost to make the experience both for his candidate and his congregation an act of worship, a service of life-dedication, and a blessed memory.

These are days when our Protestant churches are on the offensive. Evangelism is receiving new and greater attention. When the Master gave the Great Commission—"Go ye therefore, and teach all nations, baptizing them in the name of the Father, and of the Son, and of the Holy Ghost: teaching them to observe all things whatsoever I have commanded you"—He was speaking to all time, to our generation as well as to the men of His day. And as ministers and laymen heed anew the command contained in this commission, as they speak of their Savior to men and women who have never known Him, or, having once known Him, have grown cold, there will come to our churches year by year scores and hundreds knocking for entrance.

Some will come to revive church letters long left inactive. Some will come to ask for membership "by experience." Still others, perhaps the largest number, will come in that first, fresh, unforgettable hour of yielding their lives to Jesus Christ and undertaking the daily, exciting adventure of living by the will of God.

This group, coming into membership in the church for the first time, will come by the door of baptism—"believer's baptism," as the fathers have delighted to call it. In Paul's words, they will be buried with Christ "by baptism into death: that like as Christ was raised up from the dead by the glory of the Father," even so they also shall "walk in newness of life."

For these new Christians the experience of Jesus, baptized in the waters of the River Jordan by His cousin John, will take on new meaning. And to many of the group there will come, even as there came to Jesus as He was raised from the waters, that indelible, inescapable assurance that the Eternal Father is pleased with what has been done.

Throughout the centuries there have been churches which have faithfully held to the practice of immersion as "believer's baptism." They have not baptized infants; and, with rare exceptions, they have not accepted other forms of baptism as a substitute for immersion with its symbolic drama of death and resurrection. Even when some of those churches have been willing to accept into membership by church letter men and women from non-immersionist communions, they almost always have insisted on immersion as the form of baptism for those coming to the Christian experience for the first time.

In many of the immersionist churches, however, there is a feeling amounting almost to fear that their ministers are failing to administer the ordinance of baptism in the most helpful and impressive way. Too often baptism has become a commonplace service, meaningless to the congregation and an unhappy experience to the candidate. Too often insufficient attention is given to the details of the service, and the beauty that might be there is embarrassingly absent. Too often baptism is allowed to become a public spectacle wherein the "public witness" is cheapened.

Many of our thoughtful laymen and consecrated leaders are coming to believe that if immersion is to continue as a respected and beloved practice, more care must be taken to insure those details of preparation and administration which will make the ordinance a spiritual experience of joy and consecration. The willingness of some churches to accept other forms of baptism than immersion has come, in part, from public pressure aroused by baptisms that were poorly conducted. Stories could be told, experiences recounted, ugly and thoroughly unpleasant, that would give any young man or woman, or any older man or woman, reason to pause before beginning his or her Christian life in a church which demanded baptism of *that* sort as the condition of admission.

In the course of gathering the material for the film, for the articles, and for this handbook, I have had occasion to talk to many ministers and to inquire regarding their practices in the service of baptism; I have inspected the equipment which their churches provided—the dressing rooms, the candidates' robes, the minister's garments, the structure and arrangement of the baptistry. Out of this study one strong conviction has come. It is that we of the immersionist churches, if we are to make our services of baptism meaningful experiences to the candidates and persuasive invitations to consecration on the

The ordinance of baptism here is being administered to
a young candidate in a manner which is in every way
reverent, beautiful, and impressive. The minister is
Dr. Lewis Jacobsen.

The series of photographs on this and the next page show in considerable detail how baptism is administered by Rev. Raymond L. Bailey, pastor of the First Baptist Church, Columbus, Ohio. The upper photograph shows him meeting the candidate as the latter enters the pool. He then leads the candidate to the position shown in the lower photograph. It is here that he asks the candidate for his confession of faith.

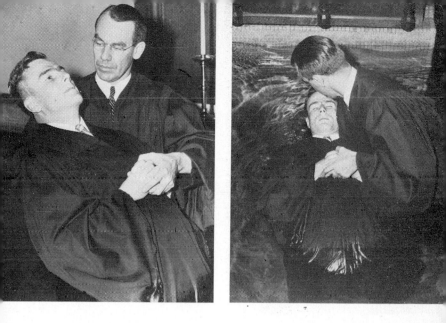

1. The minister, supporting the candidate's shoulders with his right hand, lowers him slowly into the water. 2. The moment before complete immersion. 3. He begins to raise the candidate to his feet. 4. He wipes the candidate's face and directs him to the steps leading from the baptistry.

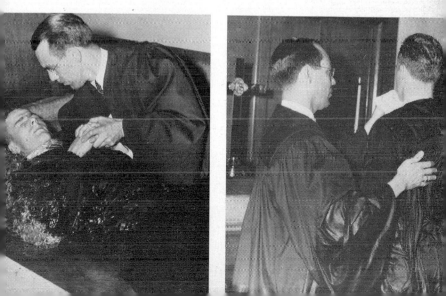

ABOVE: An unattractive baptistry can be beautified with autumn leaves and evergreen branches. Attendants of the Cross add meaning to the scene. BELOW: A baptism in Calvary Baptist Church, Washington, D. C., by Dr. Clarence W. Cranford. Robed attendants light a candle after each immersion.

part of our congregations, must give more careful thought to the details of the service. And to do this, one of the best ways may be for the young minister himself, particularly if his own baptism was in his early boyhood, to go to some respected older fellow minister and ask him to take him *in a private or semiprivate service* through the experience of Christian baptism *in his own church, with his own equipment.* This suggestion may appear strange. Some at first will count it blasphemous. But for others it may appear to deserve quiet, dispassionate consideration.

The minister of any church, facing his opportunity to make baptism of largest meaning to children, to young people, and to adults, will come to the service with deeper resources and with more sensitive understanding if he himself has undergone the experience recently. He will be able to put himself more imaginatively into the mood and mind of the candidate coming to it for the first time. When dignity and beauty come into any service of the church, they do not come by chance. Unless the young pastor knows the experience to which the candidate is coming, either through having been recently in the role of candidate himself or through creative imagination, he may easily overlook some of the necessary details that make for that dignity and beauty.

For the minister, such a rebaptism can be a service of reconsecration. Let him invite other fellow ministers, if he cares to do so, or some of his deacons, that they also may hear the instructions offered by the friend officiating, and that he may have the sensation of going into the baptismal waters fully clad and of being buried and raised again in the presence of understanding friends.

I would make these two further suggestions: First, let the young minister arrange with a member of his church to serve as candidate for a practice baptism. It will be an experience which, if cared for with reverence, can be of inestimable aid to the young minister. Let him try the various techniques and procedures which are suggested in these chapters. Let him find by trial and error the way he can best care for the candidate with ease and satisfaction to himself and with the utmost assurance and comfort to the candidate.

Too often a minister allows the procedures of his first immersion to crystallize into habits even though the choices were made with little thought. Too often he accepts his own inadequacy because he has had no opportunity to study the situation and to make choice *through practice* of the alternatives which are offered. I have worked with young ministers in such practice situations, and it is my judgment that they learn to care for their services of baptism with an ease and assurance and a beauty that could have come in no other way.

The second suggestion is that at five- or ten-year intervals the minister invite a sensitive and critical friend to witness one of his services of baptism and to report to him in detail his judgment of the beauty and dignity of the service.

This is in line with a word that I have often spoken to young ministers, urging them on occasion to invite a friend to be present at their worship service and to listen with critical ear to the sermon.

Then let the friend make a written critique to the minister on the service and the sermon. (A report in writing is always better and usually more honest than an oral report.) Was the service unified? Was the sermon logical? Was it persuasive? Was it pertinent to the congregation? Was it sufficiently illustrated with material from the lives of the hearers? Did the preacher make himself easily heard? Did he make himself heard without being offensively loud? Was the speaking easy or forced? Were the gestures pleasing or distracting? A score of questions come to mind.

Would it not, therefore, be equally wise for the minister to invite a friend to witness one of his services of baptism and to report in candor? Frequent repetition of any act can easily make a participant uncritical of detail. The chapters which follow may well afford the critic a list of suggested questions to which his report might give answer; should the report be wholly favorable, without adverse criticism of any kind, even then might the effort still be worth while for the peace of mind which it brings to the young minister.

I am convinced that if this were to be done by many of our ministers, their services of baptism—services which our churches will see in increased numbers as the fruits of our evangelistic campaigns are reaped—would carry a thousandfold more of spiritual insight for the men and women being baptized and for the congregations before whom the public witness is made.

I have talked with men and women of various ages, some immediately after their baptism and some as they recalled an event from earlier days. Their impressions and memories were widely different. One young man spoke with a glow on his face: "I feel like a new man. I'm alive all over now. The old man is gone, and I'm new in Jesus Christ." Another young man, recalling his baptism as a child, said with thoughtfulness: "Dad prepared me for my baptism with very great care, and it meant much to me. It was a part of Christian church membership, and I wanted very much to be a Christian and a church member. For me my baptism was the beginning of that experience." But another young man, reaching back in memory, said: "It meant nothing to me except a wet, messy experience. I know my pastor was pleased, and my folks were satisfied, but it didn't touch me in any way, and I haven't been happy in remembering it."

For the first two, their baptism was a moment of spiritual understanding and joy; for the third, it was a lost opportunity. Who was to blame for the loss? Was the minister at fault or was the candidate himself? It is not possible to say. But it may be asserted that the minister and the church members have it in their power, by their own thoughtful, prayerful approach to the service, and by their careful attention to its details, to make certain that for all who come to the glorious adventure of Christian dedication, their baptism shall be a moment to live in happy memory, with its own power to reconsecrate by its renewal of eternal vows.

CHAPTER 2

Baptism Can Be Beautiful

"When he was baptized . . . lo, the
heavens were opened unto him."
—*Matthew 3:16*

BAPTISM can be beautiful—IF! The conditions inherent in this IF must be met;
otherwise, baptism becomes a routine service without
spiritual light, an uninspiring fulfillment of a divine
command, a mere meeting of a traditional demand
made on those seeking church membership. Baptism
can be a spiritual drama with power and joy for
both the candidate and the observers, but it will not
become so unless certain conditions are carefully
met.

These conditions are sufficiently general to apply
to virtually all services of baptism, regardless of
the age of the candidate. In each case, however,
the pastor must interpret the conditions in terms of
the needs of the individual. Baptism, then, can be
beautiful if five conditions are fulfilled.

*Baptism can be beautiful—IF the candidate un-
derstands with appreciation the significance of the*

ordinance in which he is participating. This understanding must be in terms of the candidate's age
and experience. To the thoughtful there is abundant
opportunity for suggesting the mystery which later
maturity will partially clarify, but baptism, as an
act of dedication in obedience to Jesus' command,
can be made meaningful to a candidate of any age.

Whether this instruction should be given to the
candidate individually or as a member of a group,
will depend upon the situation in each church and
upon the pastor's relation to the candidate. Certainly
for the group of young people coming into church
membership at Easter time, there is value in class
instruction over a period of weeks. Even for adults,
classes for instruction can be most useful in preparing them for church membership and Christian
living. Most of our Protestant churches have need
to stress the learning element in the act of Christian
dedication. The candidates need to be reminded of
Paul's words to Timothy, "Study to show thyself
approved unto God."

In such groups, whether of children, young people,
or adults, the minister has opportunity to review
with those seeking church membership something of
the history of baptism and the particular significance of Jesus' baptism in His career. Here, too, is
the time to give the historical and scriptural author-
ity for immersion.

In any talk on baptism, the pastor surely will wish
to review those Bible passages which deal with personal dedication. Mention may be made of John
15:1-14; Galatians 5:16-25; Colossians 3:1-17. In
addition, there are those passages in the New Testa-

ment which speak directly of baptism. A few of the most important ones are: Matthew 3:13-17; Matthew 28:19-20; Acts 2:38; Acts 8:26-39; Romans 6:1-11; Galatians 3:26-27.

The symbolism of burial to all that is shoddy and evil and of glorious resurrection to new life in Christ—this is the drama of baptism which should command with holy inspiration the candidate's whole mind and heart.

How much of this content the minister will pour into his talks in preparing candidates for church membership, he himself must decide; and the choice will depend upon the ages and backgrounds of the candidates. But to the limit of the maturity of each individual, let the candidate have full grasp and appreciation of this act of public dedication of his life and of his entrance into church membership.

Baptism can be beautiful—IF the candidate is assured that the conditions and equipment for the service will be clean and attractive, and that all arrangements will be made for his comfort and protection. The Christian church requires baptism as a condition of church membership; the Baptist, Disciple, and certain other churches require that baptism shall be by immersion. But this requirement, interpreting the commandment of our Lord, does not demand, neither does it justify, any of the thoughtless or unbecoming practices which sometimes have been associated with it. The minister and the church which feel that no special attention need be paid to the convenience of the candidate seeking baptism, or care be taken to minimize the embarrassment which can result from the service if poorly conducted, are having their influence in the growing tendency to accept other forms of baptism than immersion and to make baptism optional as a condition of membership.

The baptistry and the robing rooms should be kept as clean as the sanctuary, for the janitor or the minister has no way of knowing when they may be inspected.

The robes which are offered to the candidates must be attractive and neat and clean. They should be laundered after each use. When they grow old or worn, let them be replaced by new robes. If the church budget raises a forbidding hand, here is opportunity for the Women's Society to serve their church in this specific need.

Care must be taken to see that the robes are properly weighted, so that they do not float on the water. There is need also for a sufficient number of robes of different lengths, so that persons of various heights can be cared for with reasonable satisfaction. Although all men and women are not fastidious and sensitive, the arrangements should be made for those who are; and the others will profit by them.

The deacon or deaconess selected to assist the candidates should be chosen with care. Those possessed of the ability to assist unobtrusively and to be useful only when their usefulness is desired, can add much to the building of the memory which for the candidate should be glowing and sacred. Let care be taken to avoid the deacon or deaconess who comes to the assignment overly solicitous or with unseemly curiosity.

Baptism can be beautiful—IF all anxiety and fear

7374

*are removed from the candidate's mind by a full
explanation of what is expected of him.* He has the
right to know exactly what will take place; he must
know this, if he is to do his part with thoughtfulness and be able to participate without nervousness.

The pastor will wisely say to the candidate for
baptism: "Just as far as lies within your power,
come to the service with your mind centered on the
vows of dedication which you will make to your
Lord and Savior. Put out of your mind, as far as
you can, the friendly congregation, the lights on the
baptistry, the music of the choir, the sensation of
the water; hold your mind centered steadily on the
union between you and your God through Jesus
Christ."

But this admonition is without meaning unless the
candidate knows precisely what is to be his part in
the service. A growing number of pastors are following the custom of arranging for a private pre-
paratory service (or a group service for the Easter
classes of children) in the unfilled baptistry, usually
on the day before the ordinance of baptism is to be
administered. If the marriage service is sufficiently
important to call for a period of instruction and
preparation, so too is baptism.

There is probably nothing that the pastor can do
that will be more helpful in assuaging the anxiety
of the nervous candidate than to show him the
robing rooms and to take him into the dry baptistry
and there instruct him in the various steps of immersion. If the reader queries, "For everyone?" the
answer may be given, "For everyone for whom the
pastor may have reason to think that anxious fear

may dim the joy of the occasion." For if the ordinance of baptism is to be kept one of power and joy, it must be individualized and by careful preparation be made a personal experience.

Baptism can be beautiful—IF the service is carefully planned, smoothly executed, and characterized throughout by dignity, reverence, and beauty. The candidate is entitled to a happy memory of this hour which the church requires as the threshold of membership. This means that the tone of the service throughout, from the meeting of the candidate with the assisting deacon or deaconess to the last farewell from the pastor himself, must be one of spiritual understanding befitting a service of consecration. The friendliness of the pastor will illumine any solemnity, but there is no place in this hour for the casual talk, the easy humor, or the action or gesture which in any way belittles the ordinance.

If the pastor wisely recognizes these demands upon him and his church, he will lend his best efforts to preparing the candidate, as has already been suggested; in addition, he will give generously of his time to arranging the service in ways that will help the congregation to come to it in the spirit of worship. And he will take care that he himself comes to it, not just as to a calendar-item on a busy Sunday, but as to a service for which he must be in high and reverent mood.

The human memory unhappily holds fast to the ridiculous and the unseemly. Those who have watched baptisms when the candidate resisted the minister, when the low water made total immersion almost impossible, when the minister mixed the names of the candidates, when the choir director failed to follow his cues, when the candidate took the occasion in nervous levity, when the minister plunged the candidate downward so rapidly that strangulation resulted—these are not experiences easily forgotten. Under such circumstances baptism is not and never can be beautiful.

Baptism can be beautiful—IF everything possible is done to aid the candidate to hold the experience in joyous memory. Too often the pastor feels that his responsibility for the day ends when the candidate leaves the baptistry; but there is still more to be done, even that day.

The church must decide whether it shall be their custom to administer the ordinance of baptism on the Sunday when new members are welcomed into fellowship. If this be their choice, plans must be made for the men and women who have been baptized to take their place in the sanctuary, that at the proper time they may be given the right hand of fellowship. Many believe this combination of services to be a happy choice.

If the reception into membership does not come in connection with the service of baptism, decision must be made as to whether the candidates, when they have dressed, shall take their place with the congregation. If this can be done and if the pastor can make appropriate reference to their presence, without embarrassment to the candidates, it singles them out and affords their friends and the members of the church an opportunity to speak their word of encouragement and welcome. The young person or the adult coming into the church fellowship is warmed by the assurance that he is wanted and that his decision for Christ is blessed by those whose judgment he esteems.

One may wonder if the difficult letter to a bereaved acquaintance carries helpfulness, but those of us who have been on the receiving end know that the consciousness that friends are sending their love helps greatly. Even so with new members coming into the church: we may hesitate to intrude with our word of greeting, feeling it to be of little significance, but those who stand to receive it know how much that word sincerely spoken can mean.

Of course, the pastor, sensitive to the needs of his people, will be certain to add his own word to those whom he has baptized: a word of congratulation upon the step taken, a word of encouragement for the weeks ahead; and perhaps a word of caution against the easy joke or the clever quip about baptism, for it is not easy to hold one's own baptism in unsoiled memory if one yields readily to this kind of humor.

Moreover, there is for the church the possibility of a card of greeting on the various anniversaries of the baptism—a note of friendship from the pastor, a word of remembrance which will call to mind the sacred vows then taken.

Here, then, are five important conditions which must be fulfilled in the pastor's own best fashion if the service of baptism, both for the candidate and for the sympathetic observers in the congregation, is to be an experience of beauty and a worthy witness to the Lord Jesus Christ.

Baptism *can* be beautiful!

CHAPTER 3

Baptism as a Public Witness

"For thou shalt be his witness."
—*Acts 22:15*

BAPTISM in its full dignity and loveliness can be one of the strongest witnesses it is within the power of the Christian to make. Baptism, properly prepared for and executed with dignity, is an invitation to Christian commitment, stronger than words.

Dr. Charles Durden relates an interesting experience which occurred during his pastorate in Salem, Oregon. In conducting a baptismal service one Sunday evening, he had made use of unlighted candles on the edge of the baptistry—one more than the number of candidates—with attendants to light a candle after each immersion. In the center was the extra candle which remained unlighted after the last candidate had left the baptistry. When the baptismal service was concluded, Dr. Durden had stepped forward and, raising the candle, said: "Is there here tonight a man or woman whose life is represented by this unlighted candle? Jesus said, 'I am the light of the world.' There is light for any man who comes seeking."

The next day there came to his study a prominent businessman of that city. "I was at your evening service last night," he said, "and I haven't been able to escape the thought of that unlighted candle. I'm afraid that's been my life all these years, a candle that isn't giving forth any light, and from now on I want it to be different."

The success of baptism as a public witness will be measured very largely in terms of the adequacy of the baptistry and the baptismal equipment, the care with which the candidates are prepared for the experience, the extent to which the pastor uses the moment for an emphasis on the things of the Spirit, and the utter sincerity of those who participate.

Some of our churches have accepted without protest an inadequacy and irreverence of equipment which is tragic. I can name a church where the baptistry is a beer vat, filled with the aid of the local fire department. I recently attended a baptismal service where the baptistry was set in the middle of the chancel. While the friends gathered, a female caretaker of considerable girth knelt on the platform, back to the congregation, to test the temperature of the water. The candidates came from their pews as their names were called, entered the pool, and then after immersion, without protection of palms or screen, marched the length of the church aisle in their wet clothes.

A public witness can speak both in favor of Christ and against Him. Some of our baptisms shout their disrespect in accents stronger than words. Instead of invitations to consecration, they must create in the minds of sensitive individuals a determination never to submit to that kind of indignity or mumbo-jumbo doings in the name of religion.

THE BAPTISTRY. It is strange and most unfortunate that so often insufficient care is given to planning the pool for immersion, even in new churches where expense is not spared. A probable reason is that not infrequently the architect is a man whose Christian experience has been in a non-immersionist communion and consequently he does not visualize in detail what is needed in conducting the service of baptism.

Recently I inspected the baptistry in a very beautiful new church in Ohio. The sanctuary was Gothic in architecture. There was an unobstructed view of the altar, which in this case was a communion table. On one side was the reading desk; on the other, the pulpit. The baptistry had been placed behind the altar, and between the reredos and the back wall of the church. Immediately above the communion table was the opening, normally closed with a curtain, which framed the minister and the baptismal candidate when they stood in the water. This would have been a wholly satisfactory arrangement, if only the architect had made the reredos a few feet higher. As it was, the head and shoulders of the minister and the candidate could be seen above the low reredos, both as they entered the baptistry and as they left it.

A point of inadequacy frequently found is the steps of approach and exit which come directly to the sides of the pool, as seen by the congregation. It is embarrassing to the candidate to be seen as he feels his way down the steps hidden by the water or to be in full view of the congregation as he leaves, his wet garments clinging to him. If this circumstance is unalterable, the minister must plan his own positions so as to furnish the maximum protection to the candidate, particularly when leaving the pool. Often one wonders why the church planning committee could not have foreseen some of these difficulties.

One wonders, also, why it should not be possible to fill the baptistry more fully. Frequently, in the case of the average minister, the water comes only a little above his knees. Sometimes the baptistry does not allow for water deeper than two and a half feet. In baptizing children, this does not present any great difficulty. However, for the candidate of average height and for the minister of average strength, this situation presents its own special problems.

It is the experience of most ministers that where the candidate is of approximately their own height, they would like a baptismal situation in which the water comes above their waist. Except in outdoor baptisms, this depth is seldom found.

There is the possibility of designing a baptistry with a gently sloping floor, or with a floor of two or three successively lower levels. The part of the baptistry where the water is shallower would be used, of course, when baptizing children; the part of the baptistry where the water is deeper would be used when baptizing adults. There would be advantages and disadvantages. I have never seen such a baptistry, but I believe that some experiments with such an arrangement might profitably be made.

Of the errors most frequently made, the major ones are these: (1) the undesirable location of the baptistry in relation to the organ, the pulpit, and the congregation; (2) the insufficient size of the baptistry; and (3) the failure to arrange for a separate entrance and exit, and to make certain that full protection is afforded the candidate when entering and leaving the pool. Each of these matters could be dwelt on at length, and illustrations could be drawn from those churches which have dealt with these problems most successfully. For the purposes of this handbook, a few suggestions may suffice.

In regard to the position of the baptistry in a new or a remodeled church, let it be placed with due recognition of the following needs. There should be no necessity for moving pulpit furniture each time the baptistry is used. The arrangement should not call for the removal of any portion of the pulpit platform. Either directly or through properly placed mirrors, the organist and the choir director should be able to watch the service in order that they may appropriately regulate the music. Finally, the baptistry should be sufficiently distant from the first row of pews to remove any extremely personal element in the service and thus minimize any possible embarrassment.

It is important that the baptistry be of sufficient size to care for the immersion of a large person without raising anxious fears on the part of nervous spectators in the balcony. The minimum size would appear to be 7½ feet long by 4½ feet wide, and here the immersion of a large person may need to be on the diagonal. A pool 8 or 9 feet in length, by 5 or 6 feet in width, is far more desirable. The very satisfactory and beautiful baptistry in the new Hanley Road Baptist Church in St. Louis, Mo., is 10 feet by 5 feet. All of these measurements are exclusive of the space occupied by the steps used in entering and leaving the pool.

The simplest form of construction is that in which the baptistry is flanked at each end by steps. See Diagram 1.

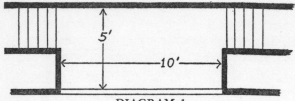

DIAGRAM 1

Diagram 2 shows a frequently found variation of this design. Here the baptistry is more clearly apart from the steps of entrance and exit.

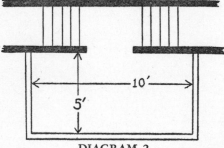

DIAGRAM 2

In regard to the protection of the candidate, let the Building Committee refuse to approve any plan that does not provide for separate steps of entrance into and of exit from the baptistry. When the candidates include both men and women, this is a necessity. In any case, it is a nicety; for it makes it unnecessary for those who have been baptized to pass those candidates who are awaiting their turn. Moreover, the Building Committee should insure that there is a distance of at least two feet between the bottom step and the aperture through which the candidate becomes visible to the congregation. Three feet would be better. Much more might be written, but these cautions are urgent and fundamental.

The baptistry should harmonize with the architectural design and furnishings of the church. This does not mean that it must be ornate. There can be beauty in the simplicity of its decoration. Better a plain colored background of plaster than a poorly painted picture of Jesus' baptism in the Jordan, executed by some struggling artist. It may be added that the baptistry needs to be protected by lock and key, so that it is not open to the morbidly curious, nor too easily available for church pageants and tableaux. There should be a sacredness about the baptistry that restrains us from using it for unrelated purposes.

One of the most attractive arrangements I know is that of the National City Christian Church, Washington, D. C. The baptistry, which is low and square, projects into the chancel at the right, on the level of the pulpit. The steps leading from the pool enter a small baptismal chapel, where the candidates gather for prayer preceding their immersion. This chapel contains an altar with a large lighted cross which appears to bestow blessing on them as they enter the pool and as they leave it. Adjoining the chapel is a robing room for the pastor.

If the pastor is confronted with an ugly baptistry which resists change, particularly a pool which is disclosed by the removal of a part of the pulpit platform, then he and his deacons should give thought to the possibility of decorations that will add a touch of loveliness. Garden flowers in summertime, bowls of autumn leaves during the fall, ferns and palms during the winter months—decorations are seldom a matter of major expense, if some member of the committee is willing to use imagination.

For a public witness strong, forceful, loving, let the church trustees make certain that the equipment is adequate and, to the extent possible, also beautiful. Finally, the candidate has every right to a clean pool, filled with clean, warm water.

THE ROBING ROOMS. For the church of average size, the problem of robing rooms is not easily solved. The ordinance of baptism may not come often, and there is the matter of economy. Can the church afford to have sections of its building used only a few times a year? The answer will be given in terms of the church's attitude toward baptism. If baptism is to be a service of beauty and dignity, then suitable robing rooms must be provided. If, however, it is regarded as an unimportant and routine part of church life, then some makeshift may seem to be satisfactory.

A reasonable solution, which some churches have adopted, consists of two small robing sections, one for men and one for women, in close proximity to the baptistry, each section containing three dressing cubicles and a wash tub to hold the wet robes. On those special occasions when the candidates outnumber the cubicles, provision is made to use the choir room or some other room that is available. For the normal situation, where the candidates do not exceed three or four, these accommodations are adequate.

It is, of course, the responsibility of the Baptism Committee, chosen from the deacons and deaconesses, to check on the cleanliness of the rooms, even when not in use, and to provide the necessary accessories, such as mirrors, hangers, brush and comb. The larger churches today are installing hair driers for the convenience of the women.

THE ROBES. The committee in charge will give attention to the robes which are offered the candidates. It is generally thought that for the men black robes are best, whereas for the women either black or white robes may be worn. Opinions differ, however, and there need be no dogmatism in the matter. These robes should be of a quality sufficiently heavy to hold their shape with frequent use, and with weights to hold them down in the water. Furthermore, the robes need to be washed or dry cleaned with frequency. These may seem like needless precautions, but on too many occasions ugly equipment and offending robes have created a distaste for a very sacred moment in the Christian's life.

I learned recently of a church that was wishing to experiment with robes of color, feeling that the black robes, while dignified, were also funereal. The red and blue robes which have found acceptance in some of our church choirs may in time come into our baptismal services.

One of the most impressive baptismal garments I have recently seen is a surplice of heavy mercerized cotton, with flowing, open sleeves, which comes to the knees. By its design it can be worn by both men and women and by persons of varying heights and weights. The man using it wears it over his shirt and trousers; the woman over a white dress.

The "New-Life" baptismal garments, available at denominational supply houses, are worthy of consideration. For the man, there is a suit consisting of coat and trousers, available in either black or white cotton twill. For the woman, there is a white robe with a large scarf which, by crossing the shoulders and tying in the back, makes the garment fit women of varying sizes. The material for both the men's and the women's garments is a thick, durable cotton, which yields the candidate full protection.

When garments like these are used, and when socks and towels are provided by the church, the candidate needs to bring only an extra handkerchief and a few toilet articles. If suitable robes cannot be provided by the church (the garments described are not expensive), the public witness can be kept dignified by having the women wear simple white dresses and the men white trousers, with white shirts and neckties.

Much the same word of caution can be addressed to the minister. To care for his part of the service with appropriateness, he needs an attractive black gown. I know of one case where the pastor's wife made her husband a baptismal gown which was entirely adequate. If, however, none is available, and the wife is not skillful with the needle, let the minister follow his counsel to the male candidates and wear white trousers and white shirt with necktie.

No matter how sincerely intended, the public witness of baptism must be judged by the response of the congregation. Is it for them a renewal of consecration? Then the witness is strong. Or is it an occasion for snickers and humor? This may be the case if the ordinance of baptism is added to the service on one of our church holidays, when time does not allow for proper interpretation, and when many in the congregation are seeing it for the first time.

THE TIME AND SEASON. It lies in the hands of the wise minister to control this congregational response, at least in large measure. He must decide whether to make his baptisms a part of the great Christmas or Easter service or a special service for those days. He must decide whether to introduce the baptisms regularly into his morning or evening services or to plan them for a special hour, perhaps a vesper hour, or a midweek prayer service, when the entire time can be given to this purpose.

In addition, by word of explanation and interpretation, he can set the tone for the service so that levity becomes unthought of, and even the irreverent catch something of the sacredness of the hour.

Another question the pastor must face is: Shall the ordinance of baptism be administered frequently, with the candidates numbering only two or three, or shall these candidates be asked to wait until the group is larger? Again the answer must be given by the individual minister and his church, and the answer will be most wisely given in terms of the effectiveness of the witness. One young minister believed the witness would be strengthened by a service for twenty-four candidates, but the experience proved an unhappy one; for a feeling of heavy monotony descended upon the congregation, the sense of numbers stole something of the individual flavor for the candidates, and the minister himself was so wearied by the service that it proved a physical strain.

One pastor has written: "Five or six is the limit. I once saw more than twenty baptized at a single service. It became a question in my mind, 'How many more?'"

There are those who say: "Let the service be arranged for the individual candidate. He should not be asked to postpone his obedience to Christ's command." A service of baptism for one or two can be a powerful witness.

A MEASURE OF EVALUATION. Given an adequate baptistry and equipment, given answers to these questions, when does baptism make its strongest witness?

When the service in all its significant details is planned with care, and when the candidates and the minister come to it with an utter sincerity which reflects itself inevitably in the congregation's mood of rededication. That is the answer.

This will mean attention to the lighting. Many ministers choose to lower the lights in the sanctuary and let the spotlight fall brilliantly upon the baptistry and the drama there. Others hold this to partake of the theatrical, and choose to use candlelight, which conceals rather than discloses.

This will mean attention also to the music. Some ministers prefer soft organ music throughout, a meditative background for the service. Others regularly use the choir for the stanza of a familiar hymn, to begin with the Amen of the baptismal formula and to continue, carefully timed, until the next candidate is in his place. Still others have written that they believe congregational singing—the hymn chosen to be one of the people's favorites—to be more desirable. In this case also, the people sing from the end of the formula to the moment for the minister to address the next candidate. Suggested hymns for choir or congregational use are: "Just as I Am, Without One Plea," "My Faith Looks Up to Thee," "I Would Be True," and the chorus of "He Leadeth Me." A hymn or chorus of about sixteen measures fits best into the time interval. Whatever the minister's choice, it is important that all concerned be fully aware of the planning and that the participation be complete.

This, too, will mean careful attention to every act of the minister and the candidate as they become visible to the congregation. But that is material for the next chapter.

There is a significance "deeply human and mysteriously divine" in the ordinance of baptism. It can be the greatest sermon ever preached. When it is planned with care, prepared for with prayer, and executed with dignity and utter sincerity, it becomes the greatest testimony ever offered. "Let your light so shine," the Master said. Maybe He was thinking how baptism can be for a public witness of beauty and power unto the Lord.

CHAPTER 4

But Actually It's the Candidate

"See, here is water; what doth hinder me
to be baptized?"
—*Acts 8:36*

IN THE ordinance of Christian baptism
the minister's part is large. For the
congregation, the act is a public witness which can
be a compelling invitation either to dedication for
the first time or to rededication for the hundredth.
But actually it is the candidate who is the center of
the drama. The importance of the ordinance lies
very largely in the meaning of the experience for
him. And, although the candidate's judgment will be
made partially in terms of possible discomfort or
inconvenience—Was the water warm? Was the pool
clean? Were the robes attractive? Was the service
throughout handled with dignity and care?—nevertheless, the candidate's ultimate judgment will be
given on whether the experience was for him one of
religious power and deep spiritual insight. It is the
responsibility of the church—the minister and the
congregation—to make it such.

Thousands of men and women, boys and girls, add their names to our church rolls each year. They make their honest confessions of faith in Jesus Christ as their Savior, they are baptized in His name, they are welcomed into His church. But essentially what does the experience mean to them? Particularly, what does the act of burial with Him in baptism and the renewal of life mean, both in the hour of commitment and later when held in memory?

In making the moment of baptism one of the great sacred moments in an individual's religious experience, the minister has certain obligations, as well as inviting opportunities, which he will do well to ponder with prayer.

1. Each age group comes to it with a different psychology, and the minister must be aware of these differences. For the young girl there are the elements of glow and of fear; for the young person in his teens, the adolescent timidity which accompanies any public appearance—that and the deep internal surges; for the mature man and woman, a sensitiveness, a joy, a release that comes with great decisions, mingled perhaps with fear and embarrassment. The wise pastor will recognize these attitudes and choose his words to encourage and fortify and reassure, as may be necessary.

2. The moment is sacred, and the candidate must be made to feel the sacredness; but the great moments of life are associated with human fellowship. The friendship of the candidate for his pastor, his respect for him, and his belief in his integrity are basic elements in establishing that security of feeling

which should come. Pitiful, indeed, is the pastor who through mistaken humor or easy frivolity speaks lightly of the occasion and causes the candidate, regardless of age, to question the sacredness of the hour!

3. The candidate is being asked to take his vows of commitment. These are pledges which are intended to be lasting, "promises for keeps." Too often Protestant churches have made church membership and baptism too easy, welcoming those who were not ready, being eager to count noses rather than to measure success by the quality of Christian living. Maybe our Protestant churches would be stronger if we demanded more of those coming to us for membership. Commitments are made to be kept—deep and lasting.

4. Upon the minister there rests the obligation to make an earnest effort to teach the candidate that baptism stands as an introduction to happy church membership, a portal through which one enters into fellowship with Christian believers, with the expectancy of joyous experiences so soon as one has crossed the threshold. There is always danger when a single item of church life is viewed apart from its normal setting, as we are doing in this handbook on baptism; the danger is that it shall be magnified in and of itself. In truth, the importance of baptism lies, in large part, in the fact that it is the first step in growth toward Christian maturity within Christ's church, and always must it be held as such.

5. Let us always be certain that the experience of baptism is more than emotional. Deeply emotional it should be, in the sense that feeling reinforces the

decision of the will; but the mind of the person seeking baptism needs to carry with it the expectancy of years of consecrated living, a dedication of will and mind as well as heart. Christianity is not an easy burden; it is demanding and confronts us with an every-hour-of-the-day insistency. Let the candidate as he comes to his baptism be aware of these high expectations.

6. The two passages of Scripture which are most frequently used in connection with the ordinance of baptism are, of course, the story of Jesus' baptism by John and Paul's words in the sixth chapter of Romans. Any adult who comes to his baptism without long pondering on the meaning of these two passages robs himself of insight into the experience he is seeking. Many ministers ask their candidates for baptism to read and study them in advance. Many make them the heart of their conversation when the significance of baptism is presented. Many use them in connection with the service itself.

Let the candidate come to this exalted moment with his mind set on that day long ago when Jesus, baptized of John in the Jordan River, came to know with an assurance beyond all human doubt that God was pleased with His decision. Then he, too, in the confusion of this mid-twentieth century, may reach hopefully for the joy of hearing, "You are my beloved son, in whom I am well pleased."

7. Consider how it is with the marriage ceremony. When the wedding rehearsal is over, many ministers take occasion to say to the young couple: "Marriage is a spiritual experience. Your vows of loyalty and devotion are said to one another, *in the sight of God*

as well as in the presence of friends. This should be one of the shining hours of your lives, held sacred in happy memory. Jane, as you come to the church with your father, forget if you can, all your worries about decorations, receptions, presents, and traveling plans. Hold your mind steadily on those thoughts of love and commitment. And you, Jim, as you wait for Jane to come down the aisle, give full thought to what this hour can mean to you both in the making of a Christian home, for your own sakes, your children's sakes, and your God's sake."

Perhaps if our church leaders can with greater frequency bring a similar word to the men and women asking for baptism, they can be of greater help in preparing them for an experience wherein the dedication of self shall be complete and the memory one of lasting joy. They might well say: "The detailed act of your immersion has been made clear to you. Put out of your mind, as far as you can, any worry or fear, any concentration on physical sensation, and hold fast with prayer and delight to the assurance that you are following in obedience to your Lord. Come to it with joy. Pass through it with joy. Hold it in memory with joy."

Actually, it is the candidate who stands at the center of this sacred drama. That it shall mean to him a taste of spiritual grace and high exaltation is the all-important matter.

I have been much interested in asking church members what the hour of baptism meant to them. For some it was a memory of many years ago, for others a recent hour. Their answers have been very different, and in their answers much is told about their churches, their pastors, and their own inner compulsions.

The comment I like best was that of a young college woman: "It was almost as if God whispered: 'You are my beloved daughter. In you too, I am pleased.'"

A young man in college who had come into church membership at the age of twelve reported: "My mother had died a year before, and I think my baptism meant particularly to me that I was doing something that I knew would have pleased her."

A young army officer, who had made his commitment before the war, replied: "I came to it with a lot of thought, and I think I was ready for it. It meant that God was very real to me and very near. I knew it meant church membership, too, but principally I remember it as a new awareness of God's presence."

A young man of twenty-two spoke to me immediately after his baptism: "I think I'll remember longest that tonight brought Jesus very near. I knew before that He belonged to me, but somehow after tonight I know that in a new and special way I belong to Him."

Here are the words of a navy man, around thirty years of age, who had sought to come into the church's fellowship during the war, but had been prevented by the absence of a chaplain from the group he wished to join. "This has been a great day for me. Now I'm happy. I know I've cared for my salvation. I know it's a day of responsibility, too. Because a step in salvation, like this, brings new responsibilities for me."

During the war one of the metropolitan newspapers carried pictures of a young marine sergeant who had been baptized by his chaplain in the Lunga River on Guadalcanal. There were pictures of the service and also an inset of the young man in uniform. The chaplain had written to the family pastor, submitting the name of the young man for church membership. An enterprising reporter had called upon the family and quoted the mother as saying of her son: "He never wanted to go to Sunday school or to church. We tried our best, but we finally let him go his way. He said he didn't find it interesting enough."

The pictures were appealing. The face in the photograph was kind, friendly; the eyes were sincere. One of the pictures showed the young sergeant standing with his chaplain at the edge of the river, just prior to the baptism. There was a look of high expectancy, of honest purpose which one didn't easily forget. The second picture showed the chaplain immersing the man.

When I started to write the articles which preceded this handbook, I remembered those pictures. I wondered what the young man was doing today, whether he had returned safely, and whether he had found a place in his church. I wondered what were his own deep memories of that service in the Lunga River. After some hesitation, I wrote to the address given in the newspaper article. Yes, he was there; he was a carpenter. No, he had never gone on to finish his high school education. Some day he wanted to be a dairy farmer outside the city. We arranged to have luncheon together, and there he answered

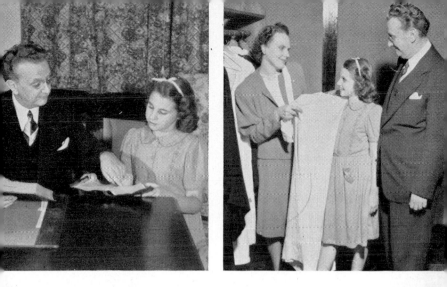

A Series of Twelve Photographs: 1. Dr. Benjamin P. Browne instructs the candidate concerning baptism, its biblical background and symbolism of burial and resurrection. 2. The robe is inspected for length, cleanliness, and weights. 3. To establish confidence, he takes the candidate into the empty pool and explains what she is to do. 4. At the baptismal service, a deaconess assists the candidate to enter the pool.

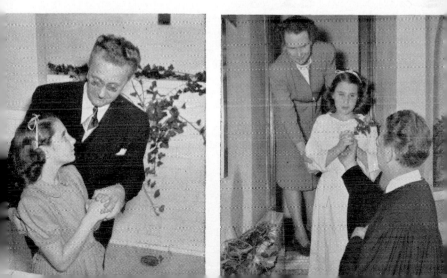

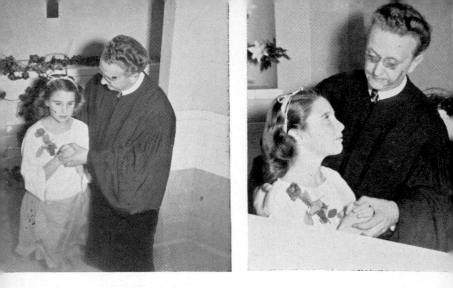

5. Without any unbecoming haste, the candidate is brought to the desired position in the baptistry. 6. The solemn moment of confession of faith. Note that the minister is standing where he can speak directly to the candidate and hear her answer. 7. "I now baptize thee in the name of the Father, and of the Son, and of the Holy Spirit. Amen." 8. The candidate is slowly and reverently lowered into the water.

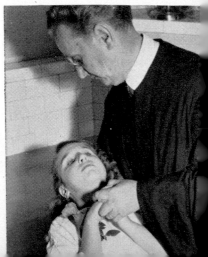

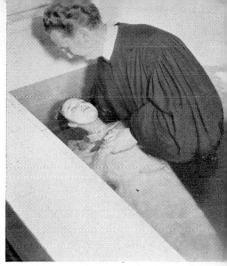

9. This photograph shows how the minister's right arm supports the candidate's shoulders and neck. 10. Just before complete immersion. Note that there is no splashing or agitation of the water. 11. As the candidate is raised, the minister gives her a partial turn and moves between her and the congregation. 12. The deaconess meets the girl at the stairs, extends helping hands and a Christian greeting.

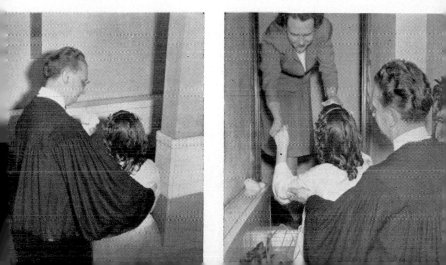

Adoniram Judson is said to have baptized candidates in a kneeling position, the head being gently lowered forward. In the two photographs above, Dr. Kenneth I. Brown is shown baptizing a candidate by this method. Third picture poses a question: should a soldier be baptized in uniform? Some approve in war, oppose during peace; others see this as a symbol.

my questions about that experience on Guadalcanal. Let me try to remember his words as he used them.

"It grew out of my friendship for Chaplain Williard. He could make me understand the Bible as my other ministers hadn't. He made it simple and strong and real. I had gone to church, sometimes—not often—but I had never wanted to join. It never seemed worth while. Then, over on Guadalcanal, I thought about it some more.

"I was getting into some awful hot spots and getting out alive each time. I got to thinking maybe God had some plans for me. Maybe that was why he let me live. I talked to the chaplain about it and told him I wanted to join the church and be baptized. He agreed; he was a dandy fellow. The next week he and I drove out in a jeep, early one morning, a couple of miles to the Lunga River.

"He asked if he could take a photographer along, and I said I didn't care. I wasn't thinking about pictures that morning. But I'm glad the chaplain did. He sent me the pictures, and I wouldn't want to lose them. [He showed the pictures to me, the one on the bank and the one in the river.] They mean an awful lot to me.

"That morning I was thinking maybe I ought to have waited. There were so many things I didn't understand. For example, Why they teach you to kill and then teach you to save life. But I'm glad I didn't wait. For I've still got an awful lot of unanswered questions. Also, I kept thinking: Can I live up to it? Can I keep up to all these demands on me? Can I be true to my baptism and its promises? I knew I'd try, and I knew God would help me. That was what I was thinking most, and I've thought a lot since—Can I live up to what I said that day out there on Guadalcanal?

"We went into the river. The chaplain asked me if I accepted Jesus as my Savior, and I told him I did. Then he baptized me. I've never been sorry about it. It wasn't that I'd been a wicked fellow and was starting a new life, so much as now I had God on my side. I felt as if a great burden was gone. I felt lighter, somehow. I guess I knew that I had done what I ought to do.

"I like to remember that day. I think it makes me stronger."

Actually, it's the candidate who must judge the experience. But in the making of that experience a source of joyous commitment and happy memory, it is the pastor with his living as well as his words, the church members with their fellowship, the church with its glad tidings, which give the candidate the background for the hour. The hour itself, however, finds the candidate standing alone with his God.

CHAPTER 5

The Minister's Choices

"Honour and majesty are before him: strength
and beauty are in his sanctuary."
—*Psalm 96:6*

S HALL the ordinance of baptism be administered only in a public service, or
may it be administered, upon the request of the
candidate, in private? This is the first of the minister's choices. Baptist and Disciple churches tend
to differ in their answers. The Baptist churches are
strongly inclined to insist that inasmuch as baptism is a *public* witness, the ordinance should come
in a public service; whereas the Disciple churches,
putting the principal emphasis upon the significance
of the experience for the candidate, more often allow
him to choose.

Although many of the Baptist churches still arrange for baptism in their order of Sunday morning
worship, there appears to be a growing inclination
to set baptism apart in a vesper hour, a special early
Sunday morning gathering, or at the midweek
prayer meeting. In these cases it is possible to
arrange the total service around the ordinance itself.

Many hold that in the case of a candidate who is ill or seriously crippled, the baptism may properly be cared for in private or before his friends, as he himself may desire. It is also the judgment of some church leaders that where the candidate for baptism comes from a non-immersionist communion, it is not unreasonable to arrange for a private service, if that is the candidate's wish. The suggestion has come from one of our Baptist pastors that in these cases, in recognition of the candidate's commitment to Christ at an earlier time, the baptismal statement be: "With full knowledge of your faith in and loyalty to Jesus Christ, as evidenced by your membership and activity in another Christian church, I now baptize you into the Baptist fellowship, in the name of the Father, Son, and Holy Spirit. Amen."

The choices which the pastor faces in his preparation of the candidates for baptism have been dealt with in the earlier chapters. So, too, have been the matters of the baptistry, the robing rooms, and the robes for the candidates.

For himself the minister faces the question, Shall I use the conventional baptismal boots which come close to the armpits? By using them he will be able to change to his normal dress quickly. However, some pastors choose to care for their baptisms without them, wearing old trousers beneath a black robe, heavy socks, and, of course, white shirt and necktie. They believe that by so doing they share more fully in the ordinance with the candidate. There is this further word which might be spoken in the tone of a footnote: Not infrequently the man wearing the baptismal boots finds that by accident water has slipped in at the top. The change to normal dress then is more difficult and time consuming than he had anticipated.

It is much to be desired that the minister shall have a private robing room, adjacent to his study if possible, where he may keep his equipment, his supply of towels, and his toilet necessities.

Coming to the act of immersion itself, the minister faces certain decisions which he must make with care. It is desirable that he think through in advance the simplest way of bringing the candidate to the place where he is to be immersed, and the simplest way of directing him, after his immersion, to the exit steps. He will have wise answers to these and the following questions if he is able to work them out in a practice baptism as suggested earlier in this handbook.

When the baptistry is rectangular in shape with steps at both ends, the pastor likely will find it best to have the candidate enter the baptistry by the steps at his right (i.e., the pastor's right as he faces the congregation). He then will lead the candidate far enough toward the opposite side of the baptistry to insure sufficient room for the immersion. When this procedure is followed, the candidate, on being raised from the water, already will be facing the steps by which he will leave the baptistry. At no time will it be necessary for him to turn. When the immersion has been completed, the minister may step between the candidate and the congregation, thus shielding him somewhat from the view of the congregation as he, in his wet condition, leaves the baptistry. A left-handed minister may wish to reverse the directions given above, having the candidate enter on his left and leave on his right.

In the case of a baptistry which extends forward from the place of entrance and exit, the minister should bring the candidate to the same approximate position as in a baptistry of the other type. Then, when the immersion has been completed and the candidate has been raised from the water, the minister may give him a quarter turn to his left, thus starting him toward the exit.

Another choice the pastor will do well to make in advance concerns where he shall stand in relation to the candidate while asking for his confession of faith. The normal position would seem to be in front of and to the candidate's left. The pastor then can direct his question personally to the man or woman. The candidate, in turn, can make his reply to his pastor, and if that reply is made in an audible voice and with a confirming nod of the head, the impression upon the congregation will be strong.

A surprising number of ministers, however, choose to stand behind the candidate, with the result that the question is directed to the back of his neck and his reply is made to the side of the baptistry. The reason for this is not thoughtlessness, but a desire on the part of the pastor not to have to change his position when he cares for the immersion. If the pastor stands to the front of the candidate, he will not be able to immerse the person, except in the case of a child, without moving to the right and taking a position which will be approximately opposite the waist of the candidate when the candidate is laid into the water.

Shall the pastor ask for a confession of faith even though the candidate has appeared before the deacons and the church body? There is no clear answer. Many believe that even though it be repetitious, there is strength for the candidate in an affirmation of faith at this particular time. There are those, too, who would argue that it gives the candidate an active part in the ordinance. Some, however, do not require a confession of faith at this time.

If a confession is called for, how shall the question be phrased? There is very little uniformity on this point. In reply to the questionnaire wherein a representative group of pastors was asked for their practices and procedures of baptism, many divergencies were reported. By far the most common usage was:

Do you accept Jesus Christ as your Savior and Lord?

Other forms were:

Do you by this act of baptism profess your faith in Jesus as Savior and Lord and pledge Him your allegiance?

In the presence of God and this congregation, do you consecrate all that you are and hope to be to a life of Christian discipleship?

Do you now believe that Jesus Christ died for your sins, and are you willing to follow the command of Jesus and be baptized by this church?

Do you pledge yourself to follow Jesus Christ all the days of your life? [In this case, the baptismal pronouncement began, "Upon this pledge, I baptize you . . ."]

Many ministers will choose to vary the question from time to time and from candidate to candidate, relating it in some personal fashion to the candidate's background.

Most ministers agree that if the confession contains two questions, one relating to faith and one to action, it is well to phrase them in a single sentence and to expect a single answer. Some ministers, however, prefer the clear use of two distinct questions: "Do you believe . . .?" and "Will you live your life in His service?" In any event, the candidate should be told in advance exactly what the question or questions will be.

There is much greater uniformity in the baptismal statement. With slight variation it stands:

Upon this confession of your faith in Him, I baptize you, John Doe, in the name of the Father and of the Son and of the Holy Spirit. Amen.

It is customary to use the candidate's name. Most ministers choose to use the full name rather than just the Christian name. Some mention the name when asking for the confession of faith. One minister uses the following words:

John Doe, do you believe on the Lord Jesus Christ? *I do*.

Then, upon this public profession of your faith in Christ, in obedience to His commandment and in the likeness of His example, I baptize you in the name of the Father and of the Son and of the Holy Spirit. Amen.

Other variations are:

> In happy obedience to Christ's commission and because you have privately and personally accepted Him and publicly acknowledged Him as your Savior, I baptize you . . .

> In obedience to the command of Jesus Christ and upon your own profession of faith in Him and in imitation of His own example, I baptize you, John Doe, in the name . . .

One minister writes that he definitely chooses to vary the customary phrases, using something like, "I baptize you, John Doe, into the joy of the Christian fellowship . . ."

One writer uses special adjectives, such as "sweet," "bold," "beautiful," "manly," before the noun "confession."

Advice that should not be needed is: Let the minister, though speaking to the candidate, use such voice that his words are carried to the congregation.

Many ministers are accustomed to raise their right hand in blessing as they repeat the baptismal pronouncement, curving the hand over the head of the candidate or stretching it high, the fingers of the hand together. A few ministers, when raising the hand in blessing, extend the thumb and first two fingers of the hand in symbol of the Trinity.

In the act of immersion, the pastor must decide which of the various alternatives are best for him; and he must know his mind in advance so that there will be no hesitation or uncertainty of action before the candidate.

Shall he lower the candidate with his right hand

at the candidate's neck? In that way he can control the head so that the candidate will not thrust it forward or extend it backward, for either movement can be unfortunate. If the pastor is a large man, there are advantages in this position. Others choose to place the flat hand high on the candidate's back, supporting the body from this position and impressing upon the candidate by careful instruction that he shall hold his head stiff. A few find it easier to support the candidate by placing the hand flat against the lower center of the back. From this position, however, it is impossible to control the upper part of the body. Several candidates who had been thus baptized, on being questioned, reported that they had not felt an adequate sense of support.

Another position, favored especially by those who choose to have the arm rather than the wrist bear the weight of the body, is the placing of the arm across the back with the hand tucked into the candidate's armpit. With still greater ease the pastor can place his arm around the shoulders, suggesting that the candidate rest his neck against the bend in the elbow; in this way the pastor can prevent any undesired movement of the head. Some will propose the objection that the minister must bend far over to lay the body in the water and that from this position it is more difficult to get the leverage to raise it. There is the further possible objection that, bending low, the minister may admit water into his boots. However, there appears to be general agreement that either the full arm across the shoulders or the hand at the neck is easiest for the minister and most reassuring for the candidate.

Somewhat upon the choice of position for the right hand, will depend the decision how best to use the left hand.

Candidates are usually instructed to clasp their hands tightly and to hold their hands and their elbows close to the body, at whatever height the minister may suggest. Occasionally the instruction is to take the elbow with the other hand and to hold the forearms and elbows close to the body. In this case the minister will grasp the wrist of the under forearm. Sometimes the word is for the candidate to hold his hands as in prayer, palms together, and close to his chest.

Probably the commonest position is for the minister to slip his left hand under and around the clasped hands of the candidate and to hold them tightly. This will give assurance to the candidate. At the same time, if the candidate will hold his elbows and arms close to his body, it will allow the minister to use his left hand in helping to raise the candidate from the water. A variant is for the pastor to put his hand over the clasped hands of the candidate, or if his own hand be small, to grasp firmly one of the wrists.

Still another possibility which some favor is for the minister, as the baptismal formula is finished, to offer his wrist to the candidate who takes it with both his hands. Those who use this position argue that it enables the minister to place his hand high on the candidate's chest and to control the lowering of the body should there be resistance. (Those who favor the use of the handkerchief over the mouth and nose of a nervous candidate have the candidate

hold their left wrist, thereby freeing the left palm
of the minister for the handkerchief.)

It is assumed that the minister is determined to
care for the immersion slowly, so that there will
be no splash, and that he will lower the body only
enough to allow the water completely to cover the
face. There will be friendly criticism of the pastor
on those occasions wherein the entire body and
face are not submerged; for does not the word "baptism" mean complete immersion? Then he will raise
the candidate to an erect position. If all of this is
done with deliberateness, there need be no sound of
splashing water and no serious inconvenience to
the candidate.

It was a Methodist seminarian, in a practice baptism, who made the excellent suggestion that there be
a momentary pause just before the minister allows
the face of the candidate to go beneath the water,
and again just after the face has been raised. Such
a pause can prove helpful to both the candidate
and the minister.

An Illinois pastor has the custom of lowering the
candidate slowly as he says, ". . . the Son, and the
Holy Spirit." The "Amen" is spoken in the moment
of pause suggested above and just as the face is
immersed. I thought the procedure dignified, but it
is possible that some might criticize it on the ground
of apparent haste and of a belittling of the baptismal
formula.

In many churches the arrangement of the baptistry is such that the pastor can add to the dignity of
the service by turning the candidate as he comes
to standing position so that his back will be to the

congregation, instead of his profile as at the beginning. If the minister is wearing a robe with flowing sleeves, it is appropriate for him to hold his hand on the candidate's shoulder, letting his full sleeve cover the wet garments.

Many pastors choose to take the moment when the candidate has come to his feet, to wipe the candidate's face with the folded handkerchief which he received from the candidate when the candidate entered the pool. During the baptizing the minister has had this handkerchief tucked into the opening of his robe. Having wiped the candidate's face, the minister gives him the handkerchief. This is usually thought to be a nicety in the service. There are, to be sure, ministers who choose not to use the handkerchief, counting it unnecessary. A very few use their hand on the candidate's face to brush off the water, but this practice is generally deemed objectionable.

If the candidate is cautioned to leave the pool slowly, the noise of the water falling from his garments can be held to a minimum.

In the immersion of adults when the water is low, it is wise to ask the candidate to place his left foot about two feet behind his right. This then becomes the pivot on which he balances himself and by which he helps to raise himself to an erect position. It is easy for the minister, when he has finished the baptismal pronouncement, to whisper, "Take a deep breath and put your left foot back." He will find that in this way the candidate can help him. The pastor must decide whether he counts this assistance necessary.

There may arise, however, serious problems when

the minister, slight of stature or even average, is confronted with a candidate decidedly heavier and taller than himself. Not only is there embarrassment for the minister, but also there is concern on the part of the candidate; and the congregation, in turn, is not without its anxiety. If the water in the pool is deep, coming above the waist of the minister, the situation can usually be handled without strain, except where the candidate is decidedly taller than the minister.

If the water in the pool cannot be brought to reasonable height, there are two alternatives from which choice can be made. (And, of course, there is the third alternative of asking a fellow minister or a deacon to help; but this choice is likely to bruise the pride of the minister.) If the minister, when he has finished his statement, will ask the candidate to kneel, he then can immerse him in the usual fashion. Unless the water in the pool is exceedingly low, this can be done without strain on the candidate's abdomen. This procedure, although not recommended, is not distasteful either to the candidate or the congregation.

The second alternative is for the candidate to kneel when the minister has finished his "I baptize you . . ." and to bow himself forward until his head is completely submerged. Dr. Gordon Poteat tells us that Adoniram Judson regularly made use of this form, believing it to be both traditional and beautiful; and word comes to us from missionaries that it is still used in parts of Burma and India.

If careful instructions are given to the candidate, and if he knows in advance the height of the water on the body of the minister, he will be able to gauge how far forward he must bow his head to have it completely covered. The minister, with his left hand containing the candidate's hands and his right either on the candidate's head or preferably on his shoulder, will be able to guide him.

This form of baptism with the candidate kneeling and bowing himself forward can be doubly impressive if there is a cross at the back of the baptistry toward which the candidate kneels. Then, rising from this position, he stands, back to the congregation, while the minister wipes his face.

Where a minister has made use of one of these variant forms for candidates larger than himself, the response of both the candidates and the congregation has been warmly favorable, and others have asked, even when there was no handicap of size, that it be used for them.

Many ministers choose to quote Scripture as they lead the candidate to the position of immersion or direct him to the steps of exit. If the choir is singing, obviously the words are spoken directly to the candidate. If soft organ music is being played, the minister can speak above the music. If there is no music, the quoted Scripture comes with effectiveness to cover the silence.

This word of caution, and how best shall it be written? The young minister coming to the baptism of young women needs to watch with scrupulous care that no action or gesture or word of his may in any way be evilly interpreted. If he chooses to immerse with his arm around the candidate, let his arm not come to the position too soon or linger there unnecessarily. Let his action and his attitude at all times be counted by all observers as pastoral rather than amorous. There will be those in any congregation who will be watching.

If the church has no baptistry, the minister must choose between using the equipment of a neighboring church or planning an outdoor service in a near-by body of water. The outdoor service, if arranged with attention to detail, can be very impressive.

It is of importance that the place for the baptism be chosen with care. Let it be, if possible, a site of natural beauty; let it be apart from the movement of crowds. The minister will want to acquaint himself with the terrain and the water-bottom, making certain there are no sudden drops or water holes in the area he plans to use.

In any outdoor baptism in a river or flowing creek, the minister should be certain that he baptizes upstream; that is, that he lays the head of the candidate in the direction from which the current of the stream comes. To do otherwise is to place the candidate in a position where the water will press into his nose and mouth.

Because of the uncertain bottom of most creeks, small rivers, and inland bodies of water, it is a convenience for the candidate if there can be two or three attendants stationed along the way that he must come from the bank to the minister. These attendants can offer such help as may be necessary, and their presence will tend to reduce the anxiety of the candidate.

It will probably be best if the minister chooses a

spot where the water is slightly above his waist, but not much higher, for the reason that in outdoor baptisms when there is a current even of scarcely noticeable strength, it becomes more difficult for the candidate to keep his feet firmly on the sandy or rock bottom, and for the minister to control the candidate as he must.

For such a service, the problem of dressing is always difficult. Some churches arrange temporary robing rooms for the men and for the women, with blankets for walls. Others invite the candidates to come prepared for the baptism, and after immersion to wrap themselves in blankets and drive to their homes.

The congregational music commonly employed on such occasions does much to bring reverence to the service. The choir director may lead the group in the singing of familiar hymns, as they stand or sit on the banks of the stream or lake. Depending on the distance which the candidate must walk to and from the point of immersion, the director will choose the number of stanzas to be sung.

The minister will be wise to start the service with Scripture reading and prayer, either from the beach or the water as the situation may call for; and to conclude with prayer and benediction. It is likely that he will need to use for himself whatever robing conditions are arranged for the candidates.

Finally, in connection with church baptisms, the pastor must decide how he will conclude the service of baptism. Those ministers who choose to leave the baptistry without prayer or comment when the last immersion has been cared for, are losing an oppor-

tunity to bring the meaning of the ordinance home
to the members of the congregation.

Two sentences commonly used in concluding the
service are:

> Lord, it has been done as Thou hast commanded
> and yet there is room.
>
> See, here is water; what doth hinder thee to be
> baptized?

These words may be followed by a prayer for the
candidates baptized and for the congregation which
has participated in the witness.

If the baptism comes at the conclusion of the
service, the minister usually pronounces the benediction from his position in the baptistry.

These, then, are the major choices that the minister must make as he comes to the ordinance of baptism. They are, for the most part, choices of procedure. But there are those further choices, largely
choices of human relations. What shall be his greeting to the candidates as they leave the church? And
how, in receiving them into church membership, can
he keep fresh the memory of the hour? And in
years to come, will the church, or will he, as their
pastor, find time in a busy schedule for a note, a
word, a card for each anniversary of that sacred
hour?

CHAPTER 6

Critical Words Have Been Spoken

"As many . . . as have been baptized into Christ
have put on Christ."
—Galatians 3:27

IT CAN be agreed that there is no one
technique of immersion to be emphasized,
no one lesson to be taught; there are many variations
in the ways our most successful pastors care for the
service of baptism. The important thing is for the
young minister to recognize the amount of preparation necessary if the service is to be conducted
properly, and also for him to choose and practice
those techniques which for him promise to make the
act of baptism smooth, easy, and dignified, and for
the candidate most meaningful. It is important, too,
for the young minister to be aware of certain generally accepted standards of cleanliness and good
taste, for to ignore these is to invite personal
criticism and to belittle a glorious moment in the
young Christian's life.

One cannot attend many baptismal services in the
immersionist churches without becoming aware that

there are in fairly common use certain practices or habits connected with the service of baptism which may appear inadvisable or may be counted objectionable by the thoughtful observer or the sensitive candidate. The degree of aversion to these various practices differs according to the beauty of the total service; and there are those who will strongly protest because there has been included in this list some practice which they themselves employ and believe desirable.

It is not intended to suggest even remotely any limitation on the right or freedom of the pastor to employ his own preferred techniques. Rather, the intention is to offer an objective study which it is believed many will welcome as an incentive to emphasize the dignity and sacredness of the ordinance.

The list of these so-called "objectionable practices" has been compiled with care. It is based on numerous conversations and visits with experienced ministers and church laymen, and on the questionnaire addressed to pastors. Nevertheless, it must be readily added that on these matters there are differing judgments.

USE OF BATHING CAP. To protect the hair from being wet, some ministers advise the women candidates to wear bathing caps. This practice is infrequent in Baptist churches, but common among Disciple churches. One of the Disciple leaders said: "I use the bathing cap reluctantly, for I am sure it detracts from the beauty of the service. I do it, however, because of the convenience for the women." Most observers count the cap undesirable, first, because of its undignified appearance, and second, because of the association of the service of baptism with the recreational experience of swimming. It is reasonable to believe that the service of baptism will increase in beauty and significance when the candidate coming to it appears as normal in dress as is practicable. Some of the larger churches are now installing hair drying machines. These will help to do away with the need for caps.

USE OF HANDKERCHIEF. To protect the candidate from any possible discomfort from the water on his face or from possible coughing or strangling, some ministers hold a handkerchief in their hands, which they use to cover the candidate's mouth and nose as they lower him into the water. Other ministers who make use of the handkerchief, have the candidate hold it himself, covering his own mouth and nose as he is immersed. It will be generally agreed that the use of the handkerchief, if kept very inconspicuous and used only when the candidate is out of view of the audience, is not seriously objectionable. With an extremely nervous candidate it may be desirable. But it will be generally agreed also that for the handkerchief to be placed over the face while the candidate is still standing erect and visible to the congregation, robs the service of the desired dignity.

It would appear to be the experience of the majority of our pastors that a handkerchief is not necessary for protection if the candidate is lowered slowly, with utmost care, and only so far as to have the water cover his face with a thin film. Nothing in the Bible requires the candidate's face to be pushed two or three feet under water. Moreover, there will be little chance of water entering the candidate's nose or mouth if the minister supports the candidate's head, either by placing his hand at the candidate's neck or by putting his arm around the candidate's shoulders.

THE CANDIDATE HOLDS HIS NOSE. Considerably less dignified than the use of the handkerchief to protect the face is the custom of having the candidate hold his nose as he is immersed. This practice is not infrequent even when the minister is attempting to make the service one of beauty. Yet the result is one of distinct unpleasantness to the thoughtful candidate and of possible ridiculousness to the congregation, particularly if a church balcony affords an easy view of the entire immersion.

A related practice, occasionally met with in both Baptist and Disciple churches, is one whereby the minister places his hand over the candidate's nostrils and mouth, sometimes gently closing the nostrils between his fingers. It can be justified, if at all, only in rare cases of extremely nervous individuals; and in such cases a handkerchief is to be preferred.

USE OF CURTAIN. A custom fairly common is the dropping of the curtain of the baptismal pool as the candidate is being lowered into the water. The congregation see the candidate and the minister enter; they hear the confession of faith and the baptismal pronouncement; then, as the immersion takes place, the curtain shuts the candidate from their view. The purpose is clear: to protect the candidate and to shield him, as he is raised in his wet clothes, from the sight of the congregation. The use of this procedure, however, seems to many persons to shatter the symbolism of baptism. Baptism is burial—that the congregation sees; but baptism also is resurrection. All the symbolism of resurrection is destroyed if the congregation is not allowed to go through the entire act of immersion with the candidate.

There is, moreover, the not unimportant item that seldom does the curtain fall easily and properly. Usually it only partially conceals, revealing at times considerably more than is intended. But even if the curtain mechanically worked perfectly, its use would still be held by many as highly undesirable for the reasons that have been given.

TOO SUDDEN IMMERSION. A study of the best procedures of baptism reveals beyond question that those services where the immersion is accomplished with maximum slowness, where the candidate is laid below the water with scarcely a ripple, where the same dignified, slow rhythm accompanies the raising of the candidate and the act of leaving the pool—are the services of maximum dignity and beauty.

For the minister vigorously to plunge the candidate backward, as is done in too many church situations, is to invite serious discomfort on the part of the candidate, and unrest, amounting sometimes to amusement, on the part of the congregation. The observer may well ask: How can it be expected that the candidate will hold his mind on the spiritual significance of the service if he must anticipate this kind of sadistic treatment? A very wise minister once said, "I have never seen an immersion cared for with excessive slowness; I have seen hundreds cared for with excessive speed."

IF THE CANDIDATE "JACKKNIFES." Occasionally
the candidate, from nervousness or from inadequate
instruction, decides to take things into his own
hands, and instead of yielding himself to the minister in charge, proceeds to immerse himself by
dropping into a sitting position. The consequence
is unhappy for him and undignified for the congregation. This awkward situation is not likely to
arise when the minister has taken adequate time
to acquaint the candidate with the precise steps of
the immersion. In that case, the candidate knows,
either from a clear explanation or from a reverent
preparation in an unfilled baptistry, just what the
situation will be; then, having lost his fear through
faith in the minister and his ability to care wisely
for the service of baptism, the candidate can relax
and give himself to the care of the man he trusts, as
he lifts his mind and spirit to the Lord.

WHEN THE CANDIDATE EMERGES FULL VIEW.
Some baptistries are so built as to require the
candidate to cross the platform in full view of the
congregation, both as he enters the baptistry, and
as he emerges after the immersion, with dripping,
clinging clothes. This is a humiliating experience
which any sensitive man or woman should be spared.
If it is impossible to change the construction of the
baptistry so as to allow for an entrance and exit
shielded from the congregation's sight, then the least
that can be done is to provide a sheltering screen or
a series of palms or floral decorations to hide the
candidate in his wet clothes from a gazing congregation. Thoughtless demands of this kind, made
of the candidate by the church he is seeking to

enter, have caused many men and women to hesitate at the threshold of their Christian experience.

INFORMALITY OF DRESS. It is assumed that in the service of baptism the appearance of both the candidate and the minister will be clean, attractive, and dignified. In an earlier chapter stress was laid on the importance of clean, attractive robes and the alternatives of heavy surplices or the men's baptismal suits and the women's dresses, offered for sale at denominational supply houses. If, however, the church makes no provision for the candidate, the question must be raised, What shall the dress of the candidate be? Too often in thoughtless unconcern the candidate is told to wear whatever he pleases—this often is too little; and a T-shirt may appear. I have seen this in a baptismal service where the minister was dressed in a collarless shirt and white trousers supported by suspenders. It is probable that a baptism in T-shirt and ministerial suspenders, if the spirit of dedication is presented, is entirely acceptable to the heart of God, but even His esthetic sense must be offended, as is the esthetic sense of the congregation, at this undignified approach to a mighty moment of consecration in a man's life. The apostle Paul commanded, "Let all things be done decently and in order." If the church provides no robes, the service can still have dignity with the candidate and the minister wearing white trousers and shirts and collars and ties. For children and young persons, white clothes will often be preferred to robes. It will be generally agreed, however, that attractive robes, white or black, add to the dignity of the service.

The undesirable practices listed here are some of the customs and details associated with the act of immersion which have been unfavorably criticized both by the candidate and the thoughtful observer—and sometimes by the pastor himself in retrospect. It will be useful to the young minister, when coming to his early services of baptism, to review this list. Then, if he chooses to make use of these or any other doubtful practices, he will do so having in mind the critical response that may come. He will be mindful also of the possibility of nullifying for the candidate some of the meaning and message of this high experience.

CHAPTER 7

Our Ministers Comment on the Ordinance of Baptism

"Go ye therefore, and teach all nations, baptizing them in the name of the Father, and of the Son, and of the Holy Ghost."

—Matthew 28:19

THIS chapter is in the nature of an appendix. In the collecting of this material, a questionnaire was prepared and submitted to some two hundred Baptist ministers, inquiring about their practices in administering the ordinance of baptism. Conscientious effort was made to see that the ministers receiving the questionnaire were representative of pastors throughout the United States—there were ministers of northern churches and of southern churches, of metropolitan churches and of rural churches, of liberal churches and of conservative churches. Around a hundred and fifty replies were received. Many of them contained helpful suggestions which came directly from long pastoral experience. This chapter is an attempt to summarize these answers and to make available the most useful of the comments.

It was agreed almost unanimously that in addition to the necessary instruction in the significance of baptism, the pastor should carefully inform the candidate of the actual procedure of immersion. One hundred forty-three favored this; only eight opposed. (From actual observation, however, one wonders how many follow the principle to which they gave assent.) The further question was asked, "Do you make a practice of holding a preliminary conference with the candidate, explaining the service of baptism in much the same way that you rehearse for a church wedding?" Seventy-nine answered, Yes; 71, No.

There was general agreement on the desirability of robes (114 for robes; 35 not using them), with a difference of opinion regarding white robes versus black robes. Many favored white for women, black for men. Some of the ministers stated that it was their custom to instruct the male candidates to wear ordinary clothes. One minister writes, "All men and boys are dressed in white suits—furnished by the church."

Regarding the baptistry itself, 97 said that they considered their baptistries "adequate and dignified"; 57 could not agree that this was true of the equipment in their churches. Forty-two reported that plans were under way to beautify the present baptistry. Of the churches represented in the answers, 78 have baptistries which are "always in view"; 61 have baptistries which are concealed except when in use.

There was a question on the preferred time of the service. Thirty-five choose ordinarily to place their baptisms in the morning service; 118 in the evening service; only a scattered few regularly conduct them at the midweek service.

There is very little practice of private or semi-public baptism, except in cases of severe illness or candidates who are badly crippled. A few of the ministers noted that they were quite willing to have private services for those seeking baptism by immersion in connection with a transfer of a church letter from a church of a denomination which does not practice immersion. Twenty-six said that though they did not object to this procedure, they had not made it their practice.

In describing the actual procedure of immersion, the ministers were asked to note where they placed the hand which lowers the candidate. The answers were by no means uniform: 76 put it on the candidate's neck; 47 high on the candidate's back; 10 on the middle of the candidate's back; one low on the candidate's back; 22 around the candidate's shoulders.

There was a difference of practice in the use of the handkerchief to cover the candidate's nose: 51 using it, 78 objecting to it; a few said they used it only on those occasions when there seemed to be danger of strangling because of excessive nervousness. Twenty-four ministers put their hand over the candidate's nose, without the handkerchief; 77 do not follow this practice, generally disapproving it.

It was commonly agreed that the candidate should be asked to clasp his hands and hold them close in front of his body, chest-high, where the minister can grasp them firmly.

One of the most serious criticisms of baptism as practiced in our churches has been the unseemly rapidity with which some ministers lower the candidate into the water. It was with this in mind that the questions were asked: Do you plunge the candidate into the water rapidly? and, Do you raise the candidate from the water rapidly or slowly? Five said they "plunged" the candidate rapidly; 144 said they did it slowly. Eighteen raise the candidates rapidly, 135 slowly.

The final question on procedure was: Do you use any form of immersion other than laying the candidate back into the water? The large majority of those replying said, No; but a few offered these interesting comments.

One pastor wrote: "After I have asked, 'Have you accepted Christ as your Savior?' the candidate kneels and immerses himself. Then he rises slowly and leaves the pool. . . . This certainly solves the problem of baptizing men who are tall and overweight."

Another replied: "Upon three occasions I have, upon request, had candidates kneel and baptize themselves forward. This is the old, old French Protestant method, and these candidates were French."

A third pastor wrote: "If the water is shallow, the candidate is baptized from a kneeling position."

A fourth pastor reported this experience: "In the case of a very large man who was nervous lest I not be able to care for him, I arranged for him to drop on one knee, the other knee bent, and I found that I could lay him back into the water without difficulty. Everyone said it was perfectly acceptable as to appearance."

The largest benefit from the questionnaire came, however, not from the questions listed above, but from the free comments which many of the ministers offered. Here are some of the statements which appear to be of the greatest interest or usefulness.

"I always rehearse with the candidates, having them grip their hands tight against their body and make their body rigid, feet firm on the floor of the baptistry. I tell them to breathe naturally as they are being lowered slowly into the water. Near the water I say to the candidate so that he, but not the audience, hears, 'Take a deep breath,' having instructed them before to expel the breath as they are being raised out of the water."

"The candidates not only know in detail what is to happen and their part especially, but they are strengthened by prayer just before entering the baptistry, I myself praying with them as we kneel together. Then as they enter the baptistry I reassure them by my manner, a smile, a word or two just for them, meant to suit the situation and the individual, to relieve tension, self-consciousness, and nervousness. Upon their leaving the baptistry, I speak again, softly, expressing joy and confidence in them. I find this confidential speaking before and after, with each person individually, to be of benefit and significance to them. Such conversation is set off, of course, from the confession of faith and the actual immersion."

One pastor made this comment: "No more do I use a rubber baptismal outfit. In physical strength

I am a good deal above the average. But I have never been able to baptize a good-sized adult (or even an average-sized one) as it should be done without letting water run down into my boots. I am quite strong enough to hold them at arm's length and go through with it without getting wet; but I know it then looks as though I were using precaution to keep from getting wet. Several men have insisted that they did it correctly in their boots. I have gone to see them do it. In every instance they have been kidding themselves. When one baptizes correctly, HE GETS WET. And we shouldn't mind. A man should get near the candidate and go on down to the water with him."

A few churches make a practice of offering flowers to the candidates after baptism. One pastor writes, "We present each candidate with a white flower, usually a lily, as he leave the baptistry." And another offers the suggestion, "A child of four or five drops a carnation into the pool as the candidate is baptized. This flower is then given to the candidate." Comment should be made, however, that there is serious objection on the part of many ministers and laymen to this practice of presenting flowers to the candidate immediately after he has been immersed. To many it suggests unpleasant sentimentality or a theatricalism which is out of place. A few churches have the custom of offering the candidate a flower as he leaves the church.

"We have found it best to have the church provide everything needed by the candidates: robes, socks, underwear, towel, and handkerchief. We have a number of white shirts and old trousers which the men wear beneath their robes."

"I have found it helpful to place a stool in our baptistry, securely fastened to the floor of the pool. Except for the children, I baptize all of my young people and adults from the sitting position on this stool. I have found it quite satisfactory and easier than the conventional way."

Some ministers believe that the witness is strengthened if they repeat the words, "Buried with Christ in baptism" as each candidate is lowered to the water, and "Risen to walk in newness of life" as he is raised.

In accord with the common custom of Disciple pastors to use the handkerchief over the candidate's face, it is proposed that instruction be given the candidate as follows: "I will place a clean handkerchief in your right hand which I will gently bring up to cover your mouth and nose just before I lower you into the water."

"In the act of immersion I give the candidate's body a swing, moderately slow, so that when he rises from the water, I am standing between the candidate and the congregation. I then dry the candidate's face with the handkerchief he has given me when I met him at the baptistry steps."

"It is my practice to turn the candidate as he is raised from the water, so that I am between him and the congregation with my back to the congregation. He is hidden until he leaves the baptistry, as

"On the bottom of the baptistry I have what I call a baptismal bracket weighing about twelve pounds—with a rod under which the one to be baptized places his feet. This prevents the feet from bobbing up when the believer is immersed."

"I instruct the candidate to bend his knees so that he almost sits on his heels as I gently allow the body to be immersed. In this way the candidate never loses his own balance or the sense of his own security, and there is no weight on the pastor at all."

"I lower the candidate slowly and instruct him that when he feels the water about his ears he shall turn his head to one side, thus keeping the water from going back into his nostrils and strangling him."

"When the candidate comes into the view of the congregation he is already fully in the water. He carries a handkerchief and a card bearing his full name by which he is to be baptized. These he hands to me."

If the minister finds it difficult to hold names in mind, the deacon may help by repeating each candidate's name or displaying a card with the name. One minister told me he always repeats the candidate's name as he helps him to his position in the baptistry; in that way he makes certain that the name does not escape him.

"After I have been at a church for a while and know the boys and girls and adults intimately, I may say a brief word about them as we stand together in the baptistry—their connection with the Sunday school, the young people's work, the women's work, or relate some family incident that I feel has spiritual value. I believe, however, that this must be very genuine and never said just for effect."

The First Baptist Church, Pueblo, Colo., has printed cards which the deacons give to their candidates. The card for women and girls differs from that for men and boys. It reads:

PREPARATIONS FOR THE BAPTISMAL SERVICE

(For Girls and Women)

Please Note:

1. The water in the baptistry is warm.
2. A robe is provided for candidates to wear in the water.
3. The pastor instructs the candidate just preceding the baptism.

Bring with you:

Bath towel and handkerchief and extra clothing to be worn under robe.

The careful reading of Romans 6 before you leave home will prepare your heart for the public confession of your Lord in the baptismal ordinance.

May God be close to you always.

The First Baptist Church of Pasadena, Calif., likewise furnishes each candidate with a card. The card for men and boys reads: